Fractions

H.S. Lawrence

Illustration by
Kathy Kifer

A Breath of Fresh Air
GarlicPress

Special thanks to:
Holly Dye, Derrick Hoffman, Jane Tory, Carrie Hernandez,
Caroline Jeanbart, Susan Rovetta, and Cecily Cleveland

Published by

Garlic Press

605 Powers St.
Eugene, OR 97402

ISBN 0-931993-61-X
Order Number GP-061

www.garlicpress.com

Overview: Math and Animal Science

The Puzzles and Practice Series builds basic **math skills** and acquaints students with **animal science**. The Series is also designed to challenge skills associated with following directions, simple logic, visual discrimination (all puzzle assembly skills), and motor skills (cutting and pasting).

Practice Pages illustrate math skills step-by-step, then provide extended practice. **Puzzle Pages** contain twelve-piece puzzles that when assembled reveal a fascinating animal. This book in the Series features Mountain Animals.

Mountain Animals Reference Cards, found on the last three pages of this book, provide further information for students. In addition, for parents and teachers, the inside front cover provides **background information** on Mountain Animals.

Helping Teachers and Parents

There are two pages for each of the ten lessons- a Practice Page and a Puzzle Page. Each page can be used independently; however, the Puzzles and Practice Series has incorporated a special feature that encourages the use of both pages at one time.

Special Feature- If you hold a *Puzzle Page* up to the light, you will see the same problems showing in the center of the puzzle pieces (actually showing through from the *Practice Page*) that are to the left of the puzzle pieces on the Puzzle Page. This feature is useful so a student will not lose the potential for the answer after he or she has cut out the puzzle piece. This feature is also useful if a student does not follow directions and cuts out all puzzle pieces at one time.

Table of Contents

$\dfrac{1}{8}$ = 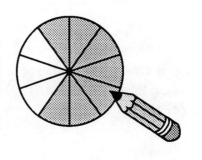 $\dfrac{7}{10}$ =

$\dfrac{1}{4}$ = $\dfrac{3}{5}$ = $\dfrac{5}{8}$ =

$\dfrac{2}{3}$ = $\dfrac{5}{6}$ = $\dfrac{3}{4}$ =

$\dfrac{1}{2}$ = $\dfrac{3}{8}$ = $\dfrac{1}{6}$ =

$\dfrac{4}{4}$ = $\dfrac{1}{3}$ = $\dfrac{7}{8}$ =

**NAME
NOMBRE** _____

Instructions:

1. Cut out <u>one</u> puzzle
   piece at a time.
2. Paste the puzzle piece
   in the box with the
   equivalent answer.

Instrucciones:

1. Recorte <u>una</u> pieza del
   rompecabezas a la vez.
2. Pegue la pieza del
   rompecabezas en el
   recuadro que tiene la
   respuesta equivalente.

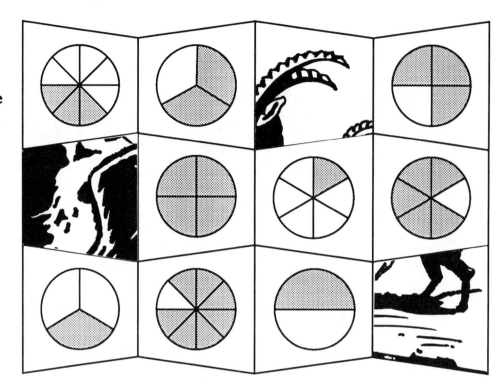

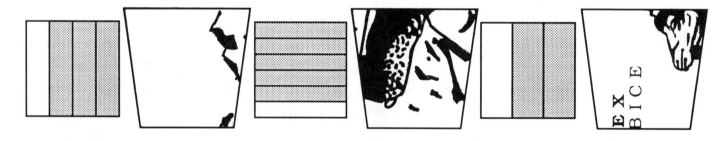

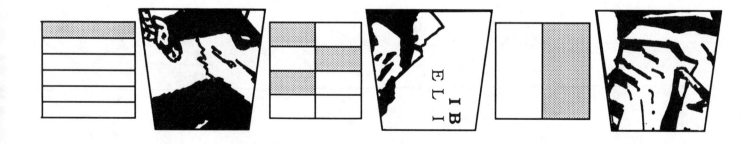

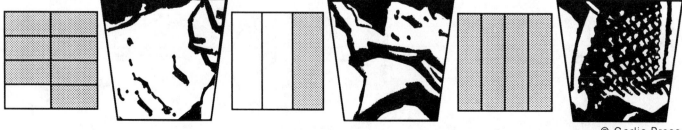

2

NAME
NOMBRE _____

$\dfrac{3}{4} =$ 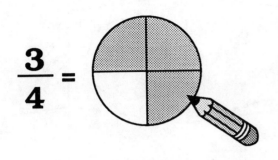 $\dfrac{1}{3} =$

$\dfrac{4}{5} =$ $\dfrac{6}{8} =$ $\dfrac{4}{6} =$

$\dfrac{8}{8} =$ $\dfrac{5}{6} =$ $\dfrac{3}{3} =$

$\dfrac{2}{5} =$ $\dfrac{1}{2} =$ $\dfrac{2}{6} =$

$\dfrac{1}{8} =$ $\dfrac{3}{5} =$ $\dfrac{1}{4} =$

NAME
NOMBRE _____

Instructions:

1. **Cut out one puzzle piece at a time.**
2. **Paste the puzzle piece in the box with the equivalent answer.**

Instrucciones:

1. Recorte una pieza del rompecabezas a la vez.
2. Pegue la pieza del rompecabezas en el recuadro que tiene la respuesta equivalente.

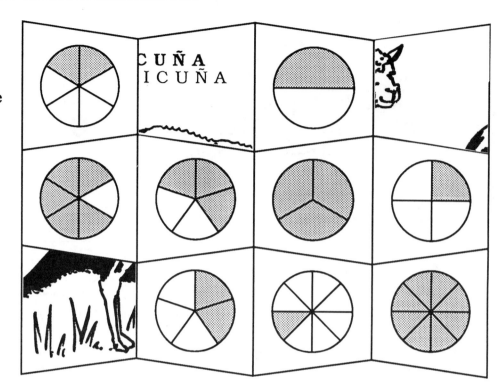

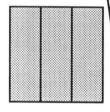  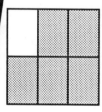  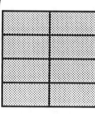 

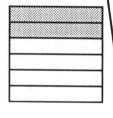    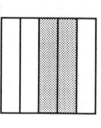 

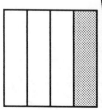  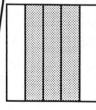  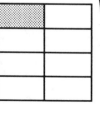 

4

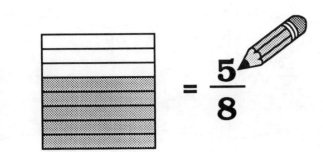 $= \dfrac{5}{8}$

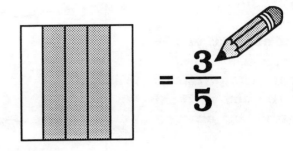 $= \dfrac{3}{5}$

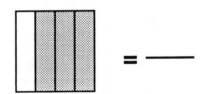 $=$ _____

$=$ _____ $=$ _____ $=$ _____

$=$ _____   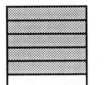 $=$ _____    $=$ _____

$=$ _____ $=$ _____ $=$ _____

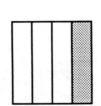 $=$ _____   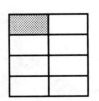 $=$ _____

NAME
NOMBRE _____

Instructions:

1. Cut out <u>one</u> puzzle piece at a time.
2. Paste the puzzle piece in the box with the equivalent answer.

Instrucciones:

1. Recorte <u>una</u> pieza del rompecabezas a la vez.
2. Pegue la pieza del rompecabezas en el recuadro que tiene la respuesta equivalente.

$\frac{2}{5}$	$\frac{6}{10}$	$\frac{1}{8}$	$\frac{1}{1}$
$\frac{4}{9}$	$\frac{3}{4}$		
$\frac{1}{2}$		$\frac{5}{6}$	$\frac{1}{4}$

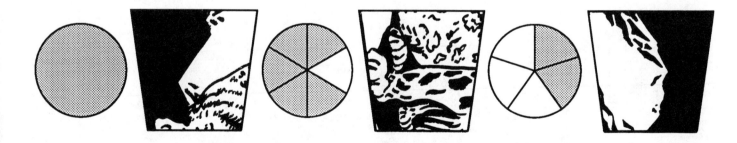
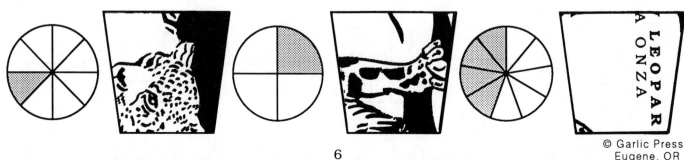

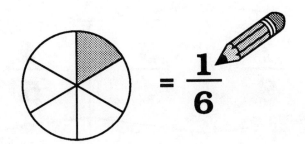 $= \dfrac{1}{6}$ 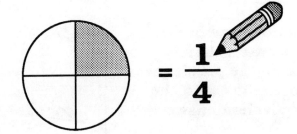 $= \dfrac{1}{4}$

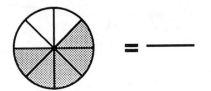   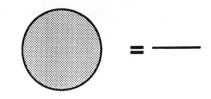

Lesson / Lección 4

NAME
NOMBRE _____

Instructions:

1. Cut out <u>one</u> puzzle piece at a time.
2. Paste the puzzle piece in the box with the equivalent answer.

Instrucciones:

1. Recorte <u>una</u> pieza del rompecabezas a la vez.
2. Pegue la pieza del rompecabezas en el recuadro que tiene la respuesta equivalente.

$\frac{1}{3}$ $\frac{3}{4}$ $\frac{4}{5}$

$\frac{2}{5}$ $\frac{7}{10}$ $\frac{5}{9}$

$\frac{3}{7}$ $\frac{1}{2}$ $\frac{5}{6}$

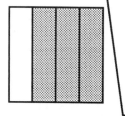 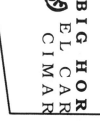   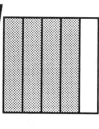 

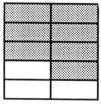  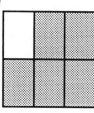  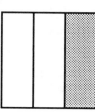 

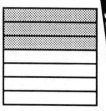  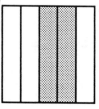  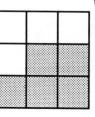 

8

$$\frac{1}{2} = \frac{?}{4} \quad \longrightarrow \quad \frac{1}{2} \times \frac{2}{2} = \frac{2}{4} \quad \longrightarrow$$

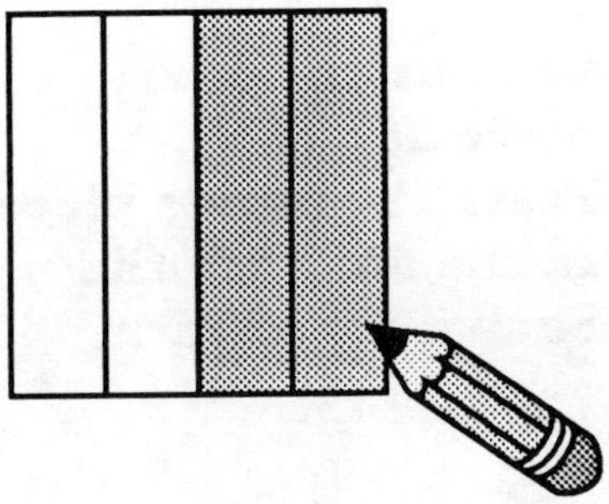

© Garlic Press Eugene, OR

$\dfrac{1}{4}$ =

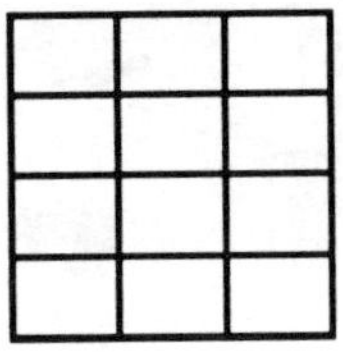

$\dfrac{2}{5}$ =

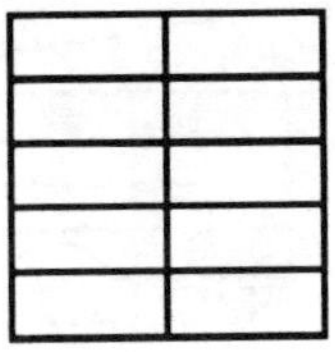

$\dfrac{5}{6}$ =

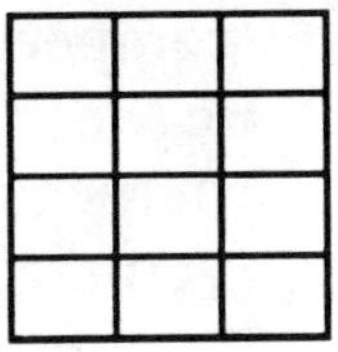

$\dfrac{2}{3}$ =

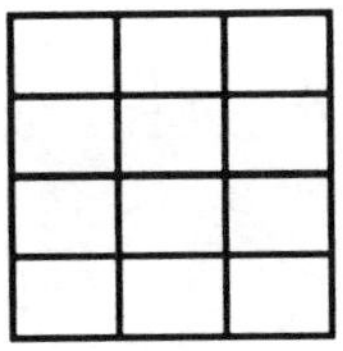

$\dfrac{1}{1}$ =

$\dfrac{3}{4}$ =

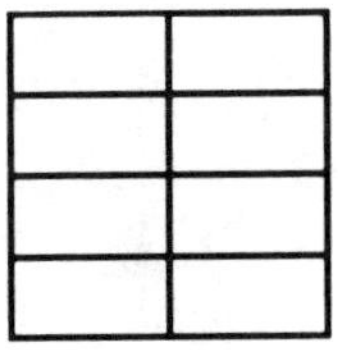

$\dfrac{5}{8}$ =

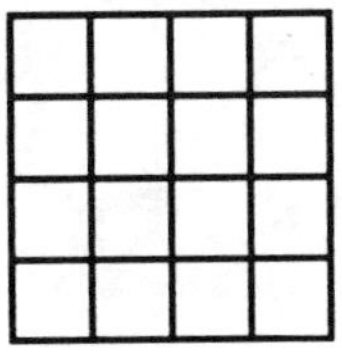

$\dfrac{4}{5}$ =

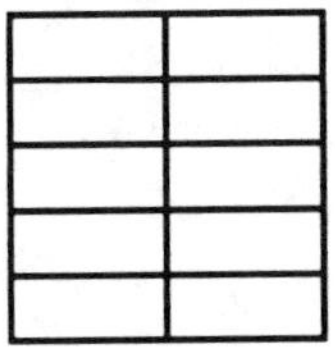

$\dfrac{1}{3}$ =

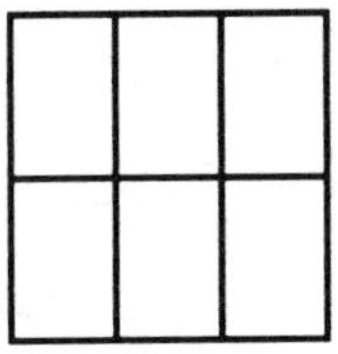

$\dfrac{3}{5}$ =

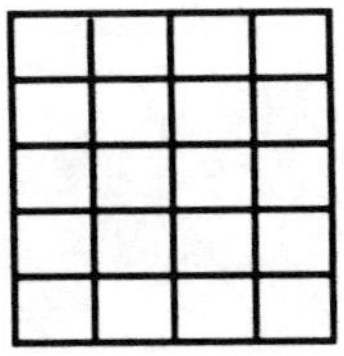

$\dfrac{1}{2}$ =

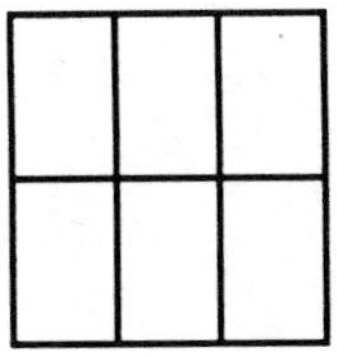

$\dfrac{3}{7}$ =

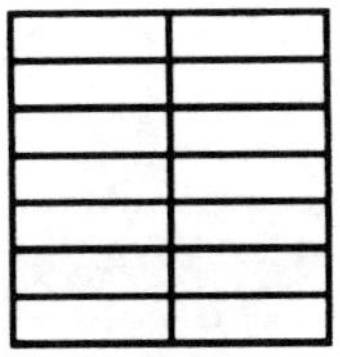

NAME
NOMBRE _____

Instructions:

1. **Cut out one puzzle piece at a time.**
2. **Paste the puzzle piece in the box with the equivalent answer.**

Instrucciones:

1. Recorte una pieza del rompecabezas a la vez.
2. Pegue la pieza del rompecabezas en el recuadro que tiene la respuesta equivalente.

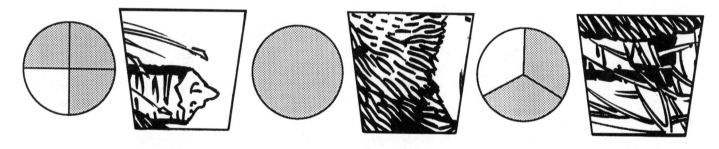

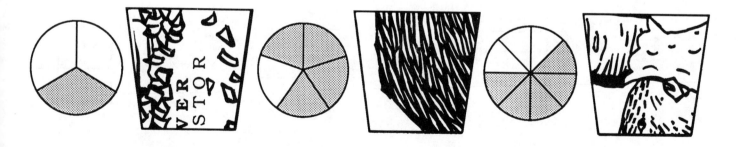

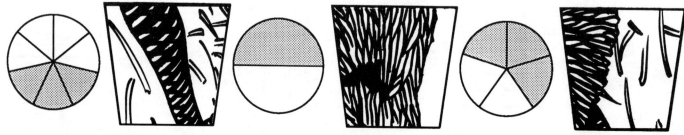

$$\frac{3}{5} = \frac{?}{20} \longrightarrow \frac{3}{5} \begin{array}{c} x \\ x \end{array} \frac{4}{4} = \frac{12}{20} \longrightarrow$$

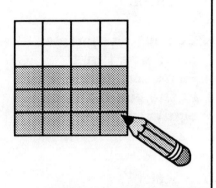

© Garlic Press Eugene, OR

$\frac{3}{4}$ =

$\frac{1}{6}$ =

$\frac{2}{3}$ =

$\frac{1}{2}$ =

$\frac{7}{8}$ =

$\frac{4}{5}$ =

$\frac{1}{3}$ =

$\frac{4}{9}$ =

$\frac{1}{1}$ =

$\frac{1}{4}$ =

$\frac{3}{8}$ =

$\frac{5}{7}$ =

NAME
NOMBRE _____

Instructions:

1. **Cut out <u>one</u> puzzle piece at a time.**
2. **Paste the puzzle piece in the box with the equivalent answer.**

Instrucciones:

1. Recorte <u>una</u> pieza del rompecabezas a la vez.
2. Pegue la pieza del rompecabezas en el recuadro que tiene la respuesta equivalente.

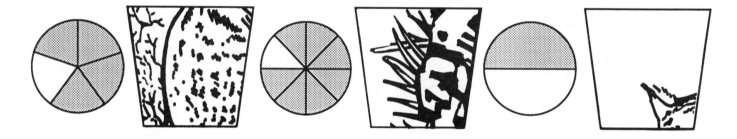

12

$$\frac{16}{20} = \frac{16}{20} \div \frac{4}{4} = \frac{4}{5} \qquad \frac{16}{20} = \frac{4}{5}$$

$$\frac{9}{24} = \qquad \frac{45}{63} = \qquad \frac{8}{12} =$$

$$\frac{20}{36} = \qquad \frac{8}{16} = \qquad \frac{35}{50} =$$

$$\frac{21}{28} = \qquad \frac{45}{54} = \qquad \frac{6}{18} =$$

$$\frac{25}{40} = \qquad \frac{6}{15} = \qquad \frac{32}{56} =$$

NAME
NOMBRE _____

Instructions:

1. **Cut out one puzzle piece at a time.**
2. **Paste the puzzle piece in the box with the equivalent answer.**

Instrucciones:

1. Recorte una pieza del rompecabezas a la vez.
2. Pegue la pieza del rompecabezas en el recuadro que tiene la respuesta equivalente.

$\dfrac{5}{9}$ $\dfrac{2}{5}$ PECTACL EL OSO $\dfrac{1}{2}$

$\dfrac{1}{3}$ $\dfrac{7}{10}$ $\dfrac{5}{6}$ $\dfrac{3}{4}$

$\dfrac{5}{8}$ $\dfrac{4}{7}$

$\dfrac{21}{30}$

$\dfrac{6}{12}$

$\dfrac{45}{81}$

$\dfrac{5}{15}$

$\dfrac{40}{48}$

$\dfrac{12}{16}$

$\dfrac{28}{49}$

$\dfrac{10}{25}$

$\dfrac{45}{72}$

$$\frac{35}{42} = \frac{35 \div 7}{42 \div 7} = \frac{5}{6} \qquad \frac{35}{42} = \frac{5}{6}$$

$\frac{35}{42} =$ 　　　　 $\frac{9}{18} =$ 　　　　 $\frac{15}{20} =$

$\frac{24}{30} =$ 　　　　 $\frac{8}{12} =$ 　　　　 $\frac{56}{64} =$

$\frac{2}{8} =$ 　　　　 $\frac{9}{21} =$ 　　　　 $\frac{12}{54} =$

$\frac{27}{45} =$ 　　　　 $\frac{28}{63} =$ 　　　　 $\frac{10}{35} =$

NAME
NOMBRE _____

Instructions:

1. Cut out <u>one</u> puzzle piece at a time.
2. Paste the puzzle piece in the box with the equivalent answer.

Instrucciones:

1. Recorte <u>una</u> pieza del rompecabezas a la vez.
2. Pegue la pieza del rompecabezas en el recuadro que tiene la respuesta equivalente.

$\dfrac{7}{8}$	A K Y A C	$\dfrac{2}{3}$	
$\dfrac{1}{4}$	$\dfrac{2}{9}$	$\dfrac{3}{7}$	$\dfrac{4}{5}$
	$\dfrac{2}{7}$	$\dfrac{3}{5}$	$\dfrac{4}{9}$

$\dfrac{21}{24}$

$\dfrac{12}{18}$

$\dfrac{36}{45}$

$\dfrac{8}{36}$

$\dfrac{24}{56}$

$\dfrac{5}{20}$

$\dfrac{14}{49}$

$\dfrac{8}{18}$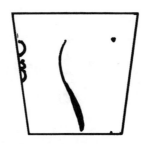

$\dfrac{27}{45}$

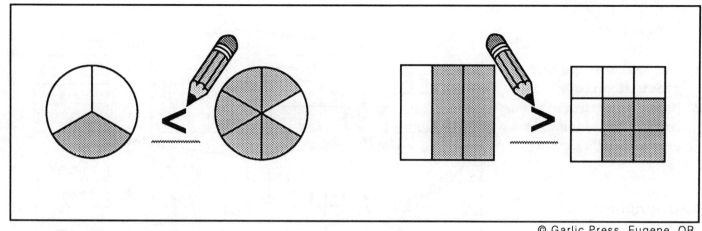

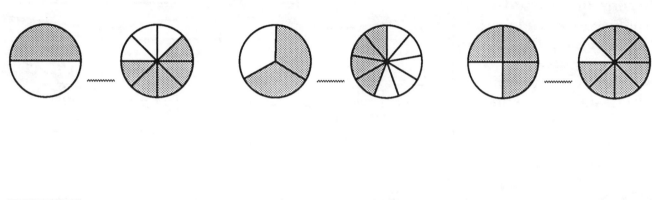

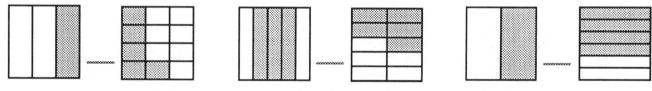

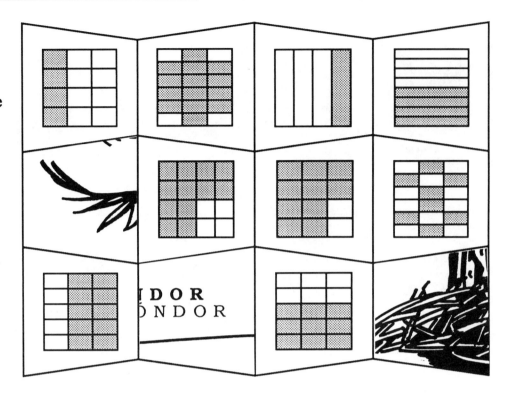

Lesson / Lección 9

Instructions:

1. Cut out <u>one</u> puzzle piece at a time.
2. Paste the puzzle piece in the box with the equivalent answer.

Instrucciones:

1. Recorte <u>una</u> pieza del rompecabezas a la vez.
2. Pegue la pieza del rompecabezas en el recuadro que tiene la respuesta equivalente.

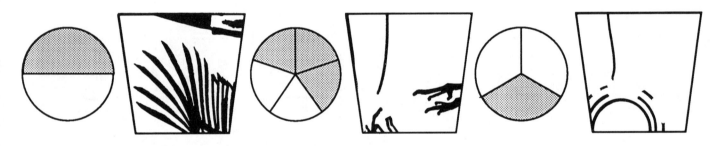

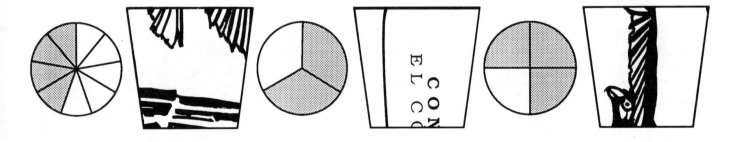

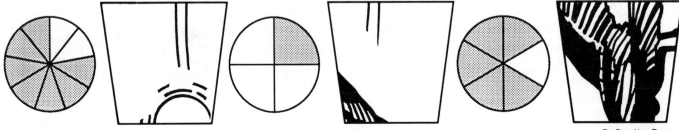

18

© Garlic Press
Eugene, OR

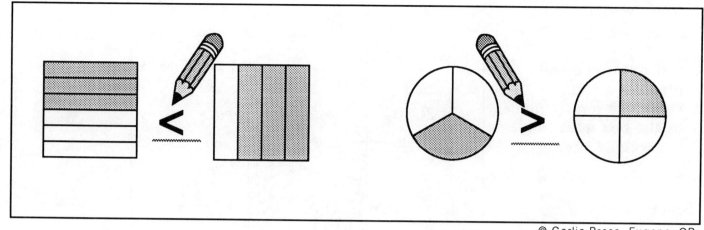

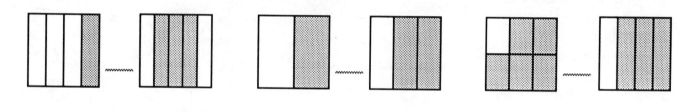

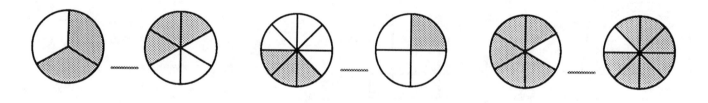

NAME
NOMBRE _____

Instructions:

1. Cut out <u>one</u> puzzle piece at a time.
2. Paste the puzzle piece in the box with the equivalent answer.

Instrucciones:

1. Recorte <u>una</u> pieza del rompecabezas a la vez.
2. Pegue la pieza del rompecabezas en el recuadro que tiene la respuesta equivalente.

$$\frac{3}{4} \qquad \frac{5}{6} \qquad \text{PINE MA} \atop \text{ARMOTA} \qquad \frac{3}{8}$$

$$\frac{5}{8} \qquad \qquad \frac{3}{5} \qquad \frac{1}{2}$$

$$\frac{2}{3} \qquad \frac{1}{4} \qquad \qquad \frac{1}{3}$$

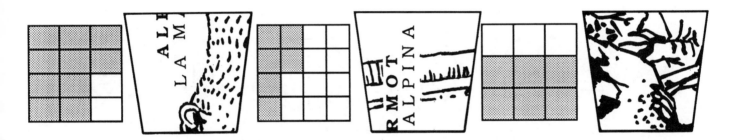

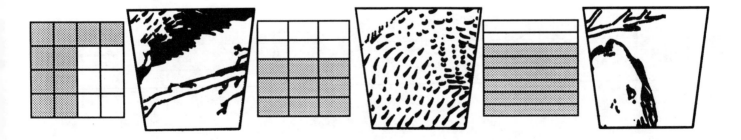

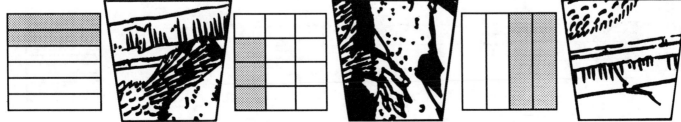

© Garlic Press
Eugene, OR

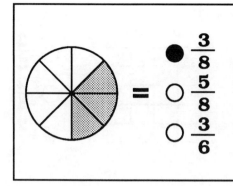

NAME
NOMBRE _____

= ● $\frac{3}{8}$ ○ $\frac{5}{8}$ ○ $\frac{3}{6}$

= ○ $\frac{5}{8}$ ○ $\frac{5}{6}$ ○ $\frac{4}{6}$

= ○ $\frac{3}{5}$ ○ $\frac{2}{4}$ ○ $\frac{2}{5}$

○ < ○ > ○ =

$\frac{16}{40}$ = ○ $\frac{2}{5}$ ○ $\frac{1}{4}$ ○ $\frac{3}{5}$

= ○ $\frac{2}{4}$ ○ $\frac{1}{4}$ ○ $\frac{2}{6}$

○ = ○ > ○ <

$\frac{28}{63}$ = ○ $\frac{4}{7}$ ○ $\frac{4}{9}$ ○ $\frac{3}{9}$

= ○ $\frac{1}{3}$ ○ $\frac{1}{5}$ ○ $\frac{1}{6}$

○ < ○ = ○ >

= ○ $\frac{3}{5}$ ○ $\frac{4}{6}$ ○ $\frac{1}{2}$

= ○ $\frac{3}{5}$ ○ $\frac{2}{3}$ ○ $\frac{3}{4}$

$\frac{56}{100}$ = ○ $\frac{14}{25}$ ○ $\frac{12}{25}$ ○ $\frac{26}{50}$

= ○ $\frac{1}{2}$ ○ $\frac{2}{3}$ ○ $\frac{3}{4}$

$\frac{60}{84}$ = ○ $\frac{4}{7}$ ○ $\frac{5}{7}$ ○ $\frac{5}{6}$

1. ● $\dfrac{3}{8}$ ○ $\dfrac{5}{8}$ ○ $\dfrac{3}{6}$

2. ○ $\dfrac{5}{8}$ ● $\dfrac{5}{6}$ ○ $\dfrac{4}{6}$

3. ○ $\dfrac{3}{5}$ ○ $\dfrac{2}{4}$ ● $\dfrac{2}{5}$

4. ● $<$ ○ $>$ ○ $=$

5. $\dfrac{16}{40} =$ ● $\dfrac{2}{5}$ ○ $\dfrac{1}{4}$ ○ $\dfrac{3}{5}$

6. ○ $\dfrac{2}{4}$ ● $\dfrac{1}{4}$ ○ $\dfrac{2}{6}$

7. ○ $=$ ○ $>$ ● $<$

8. $\dfrac{28}{63} =$ ○ $\dfrac{4}{7}$ ● $\dfrac{4}{9}$ ○ $\dfrac{3}{9}$

9. ○ $\dfrac{1}{3}$ ● $\dfrac{1}{5}$ ○ $\dfrac{1}{6}$

10. ○ $<$ ○ $=$ ● $>$

11. ○ $\dfrac{3}{5}$ ○ $\dfrac{4}{6}$ ● $\dfrac{1}{2}$

12. ○ $\dfrac{3}{5}$ ○ $\dfrac{2}{3}$ ● $\dfrac{3}{4}$

13. $\dfrac{56}{100} =$ ● $\dfrac{14}{25}$ ○ $\dfrac{12}{25}$ ○ $\dfrac{26}{50}$

14. ○ $\dfrac{1}{2}$ ● $\dfrac{2}{3}$ ○ $\dfrac{3}{4}$

15. $\dfrac{60}{84} =$ ○ $\dfrac{4}{7}$ ● $\dfrac{5}{7}$ ○ $\dfrac{5}{6}$

22

Answers

Lesson 1. Page 1. Exact shading of parts will vary.

1 of 4 parts shaded	3 of 5 parts shaded	5 of 8 parts shaded
2 of 3 parts shaded	5 of 6 parts shaded	3 of 4 parts shaded
1 of 2 parts shaded	3 of 8 parts shaded	1 of 6 parts shaded
4 of 4 parts shaded	1 of 3 parts shaded	7 of 8 parts shaded

Lesson 2. Page 3. Exact shading of parts will vary.

4 of 5 parts shaded	6 of 8 parts shaded	4 of 6 parts shaded
8 of 8 parts shaded	5 of 6 parts shaded	3 of 3 parts shaded
2 of 5 parts shaded	1 of 2 parts shaded	2 of 6 parts shaded
1 of 8 parts shaded	3 of 5 parts shaded	1 of 4 parts shaded

Lesson 3. Page 5.

$\frac{2}{3}$	$\frac{3}{8}$	$\frac{1}{6}$
$\frac{1}{2}$	$\frac{6}{10}$	$\frac{3}{4}$
$\frac{2}{5}$	$\frac{5}{6}$	$\frac{1}{1}$
$\frac{4}{9}$	$\frac{1}{4}$	$\frac{1}{8}$

Lesson 4. Page 7.

$\frac{1}{3}$	$\frac{5}{8}$	$\frac{1}{1}$
$\frac{4}{5}$	$\frac{1}{2}$	$\frac{3}{4}$
$\frac{1}{3}$	$\frac{5}{6}$	$\frac{7}{10}$
$\frac{5}{9}$	$\frac{2}{5}$	$\frac{3}{7}$

Lesson 5. Page 9. Exact shading will vary.

3 parts shaded	4 parts shaded	10 parts shaded
8 parts shaded	Completely shaded	6 parts shaded
10 parts shaded	8 parts shaded	2 parts shaded
12 parts shaded	3 parts shaded	6 parts shaded

Lesson 6. Page 11.   Exact shading will vary.

6 parts shaded	2 parts shaded	6 parts shaded
9 parts shaded	14 parts shaded	8 parts shaded
4 parts shaded	8 parts shaded	8 parts shaded
4 parts shaded	9 parts shaded	10 parts shaded

Lesson 7. Page 13.

$$\frac{3}{8} \quad\quad \frac{5}{7} \quad\quad \frac{2}{3}$$

$$\frac{5}{9} \quad\quad \frac{1}{2} \quad\quad \frac{7}{10}$$

$$\frac{3}{4} \quad\quad \frac{5}{6} \quad\quad \frac{1}{3}$$

$$\frac{5}{8} \quad\quad \frac{2}{5} \quad\quad \frac{4}{7}$$

Lesson 8. Page 15.

$$\frac{5}{6} \quad\quad \frac{1}{2} \quad\quad \frac{3}{4}$$

$$\frac{4}{5} \quad\quad \frac{2}{3} \quad\quad \frac{7}{8}$$

$$\frac{1}{4} \quad\quad \frac{3}{7} \quad\quad \frac{2}{9}$$

$$\frac{3}{5} \quad\quad \frac{4}{9} \quad\quad \frac{2}{7}$$

Lesson 9. Page 17.

<	>	<
<	>	<
>	<	>
>	<	>

Lesson 10. Page 19.

<	<	>
>	>	<
>	>	<
>	>	<

Post-Test. Page 21.

$$\frac{3}{8} \quad\quad \frac{5}{6} \quad\quad \frac{2}{5}$$

$$= \quad\quad \frac{2}{5} \quad\quad \frac{1}{4}$$

$$< \quad\quad \frac{4}{9} \quad\quad \frac{1}{5}$$

$$> \quad\quad \frac{1}{2} \quad\quad \frac{3}{4}$$

$$\frac{14}{25} \quad\quad \frac{2}{3} \quad\quad \frac{5}{7}$$

Ibex

The ibex is found in Europe, Africa, and Asia. It is a kind of mountain goat that lives in high, rocky places.

El Ibice

El íbice se encuentra en Europa, Africa y Asia. Es una especie de cabra de monte que habita en los lugares altos y rocosos.

Vicuña

The vacuña is found in South America. It is related to the camel. It is a very timid but sturdy animal that protects itself in high rocky areas away from predators.

La Vacuña

La vacuña se encuentra en Sudamérica. Es pariente del camello. Es un animal muy tímido pero robusto, que se protege habitando en los sitios altos y rocosos lejos de sus enemigos.

Snow Leopard

The snow leopard is found in Asia. It hunts ibex, sheep, and small mammals.

La Onza

La onza se encuentra en Asia. Caza al íbice y al carnero, así como a otros mamíferos pequeños.

Beaver

The beaver lives in North America. Beavers are engineers and builders, using their teeth and hands to make lodges, dams, and canals. Beaver feed on bark, tree shoots, and vegetation.

El Castor

El castor vive en Norteamérica. Los castores son ingenieros y constructores, utilizando los dientes y las manos para construir madrigueras, presas y canales. Se alimentan de la corteza y los retoños de los árboles y de la vegetación.

Spectacled Bear

The spectacled bear is found in South America. It is an excellent climber. The spectacled bear feeds mostly on vegetables and fruits that it gets by climbing high into trees.

El Oso Frontino

El oso frontino se encuentra en Sudamérica. Es un trepedor muy hábil. El oso frontino se alimenta principalmente de los vegetales y frutas que consigue trepando a lo alto de los árboles.

Yak

The yak is found in Asia It lives at very high altitudes and survives in the bleakest mountain conditions. The yak's thick hair protects it from freezing temperatures.

El Yac

El yac se encuentra en Asia. Habita en las regiones más altas de las montañas y logra sobrevivir en condiciones pésimas. El pelo largo y espeso del yac lo protege de las temperaturas heladas.

Alpine Marmot

The alpine marmot is found in Europe. It feeds on plants, roots, and seeds. The marmot digs deep burrows to hibernate long for periods, sometimes surpassing six months.

La Marmota Alpina

La marmota alpina se encuentra en Europa. Se alimenta de plantas, raices y semillas. La marmota hace unas madrigueras muy hondas para pasar su larga hibernación que algunas veces llega a sobrepasar los seis meses.

Condor

The condor is found in South America. The condor is a vulture that lives high in the Andes Mountains, preying on small animals.

El Cóndor

El cóndor se encuentra en Sudamérica. El cóndor es un buitre que vive en lo alto de los Andes, cazando animales pequeños,

Lynx

The lynx is found in North America, across Europe, and Asia. It stalks its prey of small animals, especially rabbits and hares.

El Lince

El lince se encuentra en Norteamérica y a través de Europa y Asia. Caza al acecho a los pequeños mamíferos, en especial a los conejos y a las liebres.

Bighorn Sheep

The bighorn sheep is found in North America. It lives in herds in inaccessible, wild areas. The bighorn sheep have keen climbing and jumping abilities.

El Carnero Cimarrón

El carnero cimarrón se encuentra en Norteamérica. Vive en manadas en lugares salvajes e inasequibles. El carnero cimarrón posee grandes habilidades de escalar y saltar.